SURVIVE IN THE JUNGLE WITH THE SPECIAL FORCES "GREEN BERETS"

ELITE FORCES SURVIVAL GUIDE SERIES

Elite Survival
Survive in the Desert with the French Foreign Legion
Survive in the Arctic with the Royal Marine Commandos
Survive in the Mountains with the U.S. Rangers and Army
    Mountain Division
Survive in the Jungle with the Special Forces "Green Berets"
Survive in the Wilderness with the Canadian and Australian
    Special Forces
Survive at Sea with the U.S. Navy SEALs
Training to Fight with the Parachute Regiment
The World's Best Soldiers

Elite Operations and Training
Escape and Evasion
Surviving Captivity with the U.S. Air Force
Hostage Rescue with the SAS
How to Pass Elite Forces Selection
Learning Mental Endurance with the U.S. Marines

Special Forces Survival Guidebooks
Survival Equipment
Navigation and Signaling
Surviving Natural Disasters
Using Ropes and Knots
Survival First Aid
Trapping, Fishing, and Plant Food
Urban Survival Techniques

ELITE FORCES SURVIVAL GUIDES

SURVIVE IN THE JUNGLE WITH THE SPECIAL FORCES "GREEN BERETS"

CHRIS McNAB

Introduction by Colonel John T. Carney. Jr., USAF–Ret.
President, Special Operations Warrior Foundation

MASON CREST PUBLISHERS

This edition first published in 2003
by Mason Crest Publishers Inc.
370 Reed Road, Broomall, PA, 19008

Library of Congress Cataloging-in-Publication Data available

ISBN 1-59084-004-6

Editorial and design by
Amber Books Ltd.
Bradley's Close
74–77 White Lion Street
London N1 9PF

Project Editor Chris Stone
Designer Simon Thompson
Picture Research Lisa Wren

Printed and bound in Malaysia

10 9 8 7 6 5 4 3 2 1

ACKNOWLEDGMENT

For authenticating this book, the Publishers would like to thank the Public Affairs Offices of the U.S. Special Operations Command, MacDill AFB, FL.; Army Special Operations Command, Fort Bragg, N.C.; Navy Special Warfare Command, Coronado, CA.; and the Air Force Special Operations Command, Hurlbert Field, FL.

The publishers wish to state that the U.S. Army's premier elite are known as Special Forces. The term "Green Berets" is a nickname given to soldiers from this unit on account of the color of the beret they are awarded upon completion of training.

IMPORTANT NOTICE

The survival techniques and information described in this publication are for use in dire circumstances where the safety of the individual is at risk. Accordingly, the publisher cannot accept any responsibility for any prosecution or proceedings brought or instituted against any person or body as a result of the uses or misuses of the techniques and information within.

DEDICATION

This book is dedicated to those who perished in the terrorist attacks of September 11, 2001, and to the Special Forces soldiers who continually serve to defend freedom.

Picture Credits
Corbis: 15, 16, 17, 19, 20, 27, 33, 39, 42, 53, 66, 69, 72; **Military Picture Library:** 29, 44, 47, 60, 63; **TRH:** 6, 8, 10, 12, 23, 24, 30, 32, 34, 37, 41, 46, 48, 55, 59, 65, 80, 82, 85, 89 **US Dept. of Defense:** 52, 74. Illustrations courtesy of Amber Books and De Agostini UK. Front cover: **TRH** (inset), **Corbis** (main)

CONTENTS

INTRODUCTION

Elite forces are the tip of Freedom's spear. These small, special units are universally the first to engage, whether on reconnaissance missions into denied territory for larger, conventional forces or in direct action, surgical operations, preemptive strikes, retaliatory action, and hostage rescues. They lead the way in today's war on terrorism, the war on drugs, the war on transnational unrest, and in humanitarian operations as well as nation building. When large scale warfare erupts, they offer theater commanders a wide variety of unique, unconventional options.

Most such units are regionally oriented, acclimated to the culture and conversant in the languages of the areas where they operate. Since they deploy to those areas regularly, often for combined training exercises with indigenous forces, these elite units also serve as peacetime "global scouts" and "diplomacy multipliers," a beacon of hope for the democratic aspirations of oppressed peoples all over the globe.

Elite forces are truly "quiet professionals": their actions speak louder than words. They are self-motivated, self-confident, versatile, seasoned, mature individuals who rely on teamwork more than daring-do. Unfortunately, theirs is dangerous work. Since "Desert One"—the 1980 attempt to rescue hostages from the U.S. embassy in Tehran, for instance—American special operations forces have suffered casualties in real world operations at close to fifteen times the rate of U.S. conventional forces. By the very nature of the challenges which face special operations forces, training for these elite units has proven even more hazardous.

Thus it's with special pride that I join you in saluting the brave men and women who volunteer to serve in and support these magnificent units and who face such difficult challenges ahead.

Colonel John T. Carney, Jr., USAF–Ret.
President, Special Operations Warrior Foundation

On combat missions, all Special Forces unit badges and identification tend to be removed in case the soldier is captured.

THE "GREEN BERETS"

Formed in the early 1950s, the U.S. Special Forces (often nicknamed the "Green Berets" because of the color of their berets) are skilled in jungle warfare. From the rice fields of Vietnam to the jungles of Latin America, they have proved themselves to be masters of their art.

The Special Forces were formed to give the U.S. Army an elite unit that could operate behind enemy lines. Their role was to fight a special sort of war known as "**counter-insurgency.**" This included sabotage, reconnaissance, guerrilla warfare, and teaching other armies and civilians how to fight.

During the **Korean War** (1950–53), elite soldiers were used, but often they were not official units. However, on June 18, 1952, the 10th Special Forces Group (Airborne)—known as the **SFGA**—was created. Its job was intended to be "special missions" in the case of a war in Europe between the communist Soviet Union and the West. It was based at Fort Bragg, North Carolina, a training base that eventually became the Special Warfare School. During the 1950s and early 1960s, the communists expanded in many other areas around the world. Many governments were overthrown by communist revolutions. To U.S. military officers, the map of the world in the Pentagon appeared to be slowly turning communist red.

"Green Berets" undergo training. Recruits must have at least two specializations to join the Special Forces.

A statue at Fort Bragg, North Carolina, commemorates all those
Special Forces soldiers who have fallen in action around the world.

Because of this, teaching at the Special Warfare School became more specialized, concentrating on how to fight communist guerrillas but also turn the civilian populations against them and win their support. Someone who was enthusiastic about the Special Forces was President John F. Kennedy. War had begun in Vietnam against undercover communist fighters, and Kennedy felt that these tough new American soldiers could be the key to victory. Kennedy himself formally gave them their first green berets, and from that moment their unofficial title was born. Special Forces teams were sent to Vietnam.

Meanwhile, other "Green Berets" were sent to Africa, the Middle

A captain of the 5th Special Forces Group in Vietnam, armed with a .30-caliber M2 carbine.

"Green Berets" in Vietnam worked closely with Vietnamese civilians, often using only 450 words of Vietnamese to communicate.

East, and Latin America. In all these places, the "Green Berets" became experts in jungle warfare and survival.

Yet it was in Vietnam that the "Green Berets" were most famous. One of their most important jobs was training South Vietnamese military forces and civilians to fight the Vietnamese communists, known as the **Viet Cong** (VC). But they were not only there to help people fight. They also helped the South Vietnamese people to live better lives and have better facilities. This was intended to make sure the Vietnamese supported the United States more than they supported the Viet Cong. The Special Forces achieved incredible things. They created 129 churches, 110 hospitals, 1,003 classrooms, 398 medical clinics, 272 markets, 6,436 wells, 1,500 miles of road, 14,934 transportation depots, and provided support for half a million refugees.

THE VIET CONG—JUNGLE WARRIORS

In the Vietnam War, the "Green Beret's" enemy was also expert in jungle survival and warfare. The Viet Cong dug hundreds of miles of tunnels deep beneath the jungle. They used these as bases from which to launch ambushes. Like ghosts, they would emerge from the tunnels, fire at U.S. troops, and then disappear back underground. These tunnels were incredibly hard to find. Special Forces soldiers had to track down the entrances and then crawl underground with a pistol and flashlight. Such operations required nerves of steel.

However, the "Green Berets" were also tough warriors, and they took the fight to the Viet Cong with incredible skill and ruthlessness. Teamed up with the Vietnamese people they had trained, the "Green Berets" went deep into the jungle-covered mountains and destroyed enemy bases with lightning speed before disappearing back into the undergrowth as if they had never existed. The communists fought back. On one occasion, 1,000 VC guerrillas came together to assault the Special Forces camp at Nam Dong, a remote base far from any support. The attack began at 2:30 A.M. on July 6, 1964. Within hours the camp was ablaze as white phosphorus shells—a ferocious explosive that sends out showers of white flame—rained down on the base. Two hours later, a helicopter gunship arrived ahead of reinforcements. Inside the camp, 55 soldiers lay dead with another 65 wounded, but Captain Roger Donlon, a Special Forces commander, continued to lead the fight, despite being wounded in the stomach. His bravery and outstanding leadership won him the Congressional Medal of Honor.

The Special Forces not only knew how to take the war to the VC, but also succeeded in turning the tactics of guerrilla warfare against the enemy. Patrols were sent out to act like bait to the VC. When the communists ambushed the patrols, they themselves fell into a trap set by the Special Forces. Another special job for the "Green Berets" was rescuing U.S. soldiers from the hands of the communists, particularly airmen who had been shot down. This program was called "**Bright Light**." There were two types of "Bright Light" mission. The first was designed to recover personnel who found themselves evading capture behind the

A "Green Beret" instructor shows his soldiers a booby trap in Vietnam. About 30 percent of U.S. casualties were the result of booby traps.

enemy lines ("evaders"). The second type was aimed at rescuing prisoners of war.

Overall, the **Vietnam War** showed the world what elite jungle warriors the "Green Berets" really were. But Vietnam was not the only place where they were in action. In 1961, "Green Berets" had begun conducting military operations in Latin America. Like in Vietnam, the Special Forces in Latin America were mainly there to train local soldiers to fight more effectively. From 1955 to 1969, U.S. aid helped establish Peruvian commando battalions, Chilean Special Forces and Airborne units, as well as Special Forces (Airborne) groups and elite infantry in the Dominican Republic, Venezuela, Bolivia, and Colombia. Many of these countries also raised police commando units for urban counterterrorist operations.

Another unit to emerge from the Special Forces was one specialized in counterterrorism and hostage-rescue. This secret unit was designed to be similar to the elite British force, the Special Air Service (SAS). It specializes in daring undercover operations against terrorists, and also fast action to release hostages held at gunpoint.

Throughout the 1970s and 1980s, the Special Forces found themselves conducting many secret operations into Latin America

The "Green Berets" can fight anywhere. Here, a Special Forces soldier prepares to open fire in the deserts of Kuwait during the Gulf War.

President Kennedy called the green beret worn by Special Forces "a symbol of excellence, a badge of courage, a mark of distinction in the fight for freedom."

against communist governments or guerrillas. The "Green Berets" were also involved in the 1983 invasion of Grenada and the 1991 Gulf War. In Grenada, a secret unit was given the job of assaulting Richmond Hill Prison on the western side of the island and rescuing the prisoners, who would then be evacuated by helicopter. Unfortunately, the helicopter assault was delayed and by the time the unit reached the prison the opposition had fully alerted their antiaircraft batteries. One UH-60 Black Hawk helicopter was shot down and the rest driven off by the hail of fire, bringing the unit's involvement in Operation "Urgent Fury" to a difficult end.

After Iraq had invaded Kuwait on August 2, 1990, U.S. Special Forces were among the first units to be deployed to Saudi Arabia as part of Operation "**Desert Shield**." Immediately they began training for operations deep inside Iraqi territory. They also trained personnel from the Saudi armed forces and the Kuwaiti resistance. The latter were taught how to ambush Iraqi units inside Kuwait, and to collect and pass on important intelligence.

Before the Allied land assault began on February 24, 1991, American Special Forces had gone into enemy territory in Iraq and Kuwait and were conducting a wide variety of missions. These included destroying Iraqi radars to protect the Allied fighters and bombers, which were attacking the Iraqi army. In addition, Special Forces teams also saved Allied aircrew who had been shot down, reaching them before Iraqi forces and then guarding them until they could be evacuated by helicopter. Other roles included sabotage, ambushes, and intelligence gathering. The Special Forces **fast-attack vehicle** was first used operationally in the Gulf War. This is a rugged buggy that can be driven at high speeds across the tough desert landscape. It was armed with machine guns, grenade launchers, and

THE JUNGLE SPECIALISTS

The "Green Berets" in Vietnam often beat the guerillas at their own game, owing to the Berets' unrivaled knowledge of jungle warfare. Since they were created, they have fought in many of the world's jungles against a number of different armies. As well as having to fight the enemy, they had to learn how to survive the dangers of the jungle itself.

By the end of the Vietnam war, 17 members of the Special Forces group had been awarded the Congressional Medal of Honor.

other weapons, and the Special Forces used it to devastating effect against Iraqi positions.

Today, the "Green Berets" are on standby, ready to respond to any emergency, such as the terrorist attacks on New York and Washington D.C. in September 2001. The John F. Kennedy Special Warfare Center and School (SWCS) oversees all aspects of "Green Beret" training. Because of their history of fighting in the jungle, all "Green Berets" are trained here to become experts in jungle warfare. They are taught to hunt the enemy through thick undergrowth, moving as silently as a stalking tiger. They are also taught how to survive in the hostile jungle climate. This is very important since their missions can mean they can be cut off from support for many weeks. Resilient, highly trained, and lethal, they are the ultimate jungle warriors.

TERRAIN

The popular image of tropical regions is thick jungle crawling with every type of danger imaginable. In reality, there are different kinds of tropical climates, most of which contain an abundance of water, as well as plant and animal food.

The "Green Berets" are familiar with four tropical climates: **rainforests**, semievergreen seasonal forests, tropical scrub and thorn forests, and tropical **savannas**. The jungle provides the Special Forces soldier with all the things he or she needs to maintain life: water, food, and an ample supply of materials for building shelters.

When we think of jungle, we often think of the rainforest. Rainforests are found in South America, Asia, Africa, and even tropical Australia. As the name suggests, these forests have a lot of rainfall—more than six feet (1.8 m) of rain each year. This gives the rainforest a hot, steamy climate. These are the ideal conditions for plants to grow, and rainforests produce more plants than anywhere else in the world.

Temperatures in the rainforest are generally high, and average temperatures reach between 79 and 86°F (26°C and 30°C) . This is because the densely packed branches at the top of the trees filter sunlight and reduce wind movement—the air becomes hot and still. The forest floor is actually clearer than people usually think, because

Walking through a jungle can be incredibly slow. Branches, leaves, and vines often need to be hacked down with a machete.

the lack of sunlight stops many plants from growing there. However, on riverbanks or in clearings, where sunlight reaches the ground, there is a dense growth of plants, which is often impenetrable. There is also an abundance of climbing plants, which usually hang like cables or loops from the trees. Most plants that grow in the rainforests are woody and are comparable in size to trees. Bamboos, which are really grasses, grow to very large proportions in the rainforests: as high as 80 feet (24 m) in some cases, with thick stalks that can contain drinkable water. They usually grow in dense thickets, and it is almost impossible to move through them.

There is no winter or spring in the rainforest; this means that the vegetation looks the same at any time of the year. Around the fringes of the forest, where there are clearings and areas of abandoned

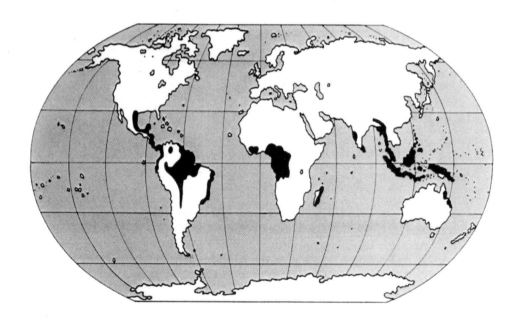

The black areas of this map of the Earth show where most of the world's rainforests can be found.

A jungle patrol crosses a swamp. Swamps occur when water cannot drain away from the land because of poor drainage in the soil.

houses, there are many edible plants. However, in the middle of the virgin forest, where the trees are very tall, and the fruits and nuts are out of reach, finding food is more difficult. There are mountainous regions in all major areas of rainforest. The higher you go in the rainforest, the more rain you get.

Other types of jungle are the **monsoon** forests and the semi-evergreen seasonal forest. These two types are essentially the same.

This "Green Beret" is equipped with M81 woodland-pattern camouflage, green beret featuring the unit badge, and M16 rifle.

The monsoon forest has trees that shed their leaves in the dry season. This type of forest is most evident in Southeast Asia and is characterized by teak trees and bamboo thickets. The semievergreen seasonal forests found in Central and South America and Africa are similar to the monsoon forests. There are two layers of trees, an upper layer 60 to 80 feet (18–24 m) high and a lower layer 20 to 45 feet (6–13.5 m) high. There is a seasonal drought, which causes the leaves to fall, and a monsoon season.

The monsoons of India, Burma, and Southeast Asia are of two types: the dry monsoon and the wet monsoon. The dry monsoon takes place from November to April, when the northern winds from central Asia bring long periods of clear weather and sparse rainfall. The wet monsoon takes place between May and October, when the

TROPICAL RAINS

Tropical rains bring new dangers. Rivers are unable to contain the rush of water, so flash floods occur that sweep away trees, houses, and people. The sudden rush of water can also mix with soil to create mudslides. Bear this in mind when you are finding a place to build a shelter. (Avoid steep slopes or banks.) Sometimes the rain can be so hard that it creates problems with breathing. To overcome this, cup your hands over your nose and mouth—as if you are about to shout—and bend over so that your back is facing the rainfall.

southern winds bring heavy rain that lasts for days or weeks at a time. This rain causes the foliage to reappear overnight.

Tropical scrub and thorn forests do not have monsoons. There is a definite dry season, which causes the leaves to fall off the trees, and rains fall mainly as downpours from thunderstorms. The average height of trees is 20 to 30 feet (6–9 m). Plants with thorns are the most common type, and this makes movement difficult for the Special Forces soldier. This type of forest is found in parts of Central and South America, southern Africa, India, and northern Australia.

Another type of tropical environment is the tropical savanna. These are found only in South America and Africa. The savanna looks like a broad, grassy meadow with trees spaced at wide intervals. The grasses can be very tall and form bunches, with spaces between each grass plant. The soil is frequently red, and

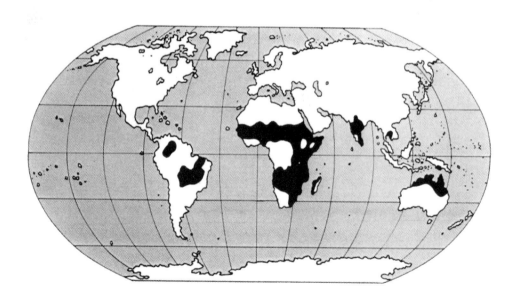

The black areas of this map show where the world's savannas are found. Most of them are in Africa.

Recruit training is extremely tough. The failure rate to enter the U.S. Special Forces runs in the region of 70 to 80 percent.

scattered trees look stunted. There is a wet season in the first half of the year and a dry season in the second half. Rainfall each year is somewhere in the region of 31 to 59 inches (77.5–150 cm). Rain falls in about October to March in the southern hemisphere and April to September in the northern. Temperatures are between 50°F (10°C) and 68°F (20°C) in the dry season; 68°F (20°C) and 86°F (30°C) in the wet season. One thing a "Green Beret" needs to watch out for in this type of place are **bushfires**. These are common in the dry season, and they can burn with incredible speed and power.

Finally, the "Green Berets" are also experts at operating in **swamps**. Swamps fall into three types: saltwater, mangrove, and freshwater. Saltwater swamps occur on the coast in places that flood with seawater when the tide comes in. Mangrove swamps, as the name suggests, are filled with mangrove trees, which have tangled roots, both above and below the water. (These can make traveling by raft and boat difficult.) Many of the animals that populate these areas are dangerous or unpleasant, such as **leeches**, stinging insects, and crocodiles and caimans. The tides in these areas might rise by as much as 40 feet (12 m). Freshwater swamps can be found in low-lying inland areas. Freshwater swamps are mostly near rivers that supply the water for them. The water flows slowly through the abundant vegetation, and these areas are difficult to navigate. Often dotted with islands, they are a mass of thorny undergrowth, reeds, grasses, and palms.

The tropics present hazards in the form of infested swamps, bushfire, poisonous plants, and deadly wildlife, but are rich in nutritious vegetation, hidden sources of water, and possibilities for shelter. The "Green Berets" don't have to know everything about the tropical jungles, but some information is vital. Most important, they have to know what the climate will throw at them. Here is a quick check list:

• High temperatures and sweltering humidity.
• Heavy rainfall, which is often accompanied by thunder and lightning. This causes rivers to rise rapidly and turns them into raging torrents.

- Hurricanes, cyclones, and typhoons develop over sea areas and rush inland, resulting in tidal waves and devastation.
- There is a "dry" season (during which it rains only once a day) and a monsoon season (when it can rain for days or weeks continuously).
- Tropical day and night are of equal length.

Armed with this information, "Green Berets" can prepare themselves for most survival problems. Their first problem is how to move through the dense undergrowth of the jungle swiftly, efficiently, and, if need be, silently.

Navigating wetland terrain can be difficult for soldiers at the best of times. Carrying an injured comrade makes it tougher still.

MOVEMENT AND SIGNALING

In Vietnam, the "Green Berets" were excellent at moving through the jungle for long distances. In a survival situation, you will need to understand the same principles of movement if you are to reach safety.

Jungles are difficult and dangerous places through which to travel. Before stranded "Green Berets" decide to move through the jungle, they first consider their chances of being found and rescued if they stay where they are. As a survivor, you do not want to travel if this is unnecessary. Food and water should not be a problem where you are; they usually abound in the jungle. Moving through the jungle can be slow and exhausting. Are you in the right physical shape to tackle the journey?

Ideally, to be rescued, you should stay in one place. However, the dense jungle canopy will make it difficult for any rescuers in planes or helicopters to see you. Travel may be the only realistic way of being found. Owing to the number of obstacles and potential danger from animals, travel in the jungle must be undertaken with great care and planning.

The first thing a "Green Beret" does is try to work out his or her present location. If you land in the jungle by parachute, make a note of rivers and other landmarks before you enter the trees. Use

"Green Berets" travel as light as possible in the jungle. They should not carry more than 30 pounds (14 kg) in weight.

your compass to set a course and follow it as closely as possible. Jungle tracks may not be on your course but will be much easier to follow than hacking through dense bush. Take a bearing on a landmark that you can keep in sight, and then choose another one after it, and so on.

If you want to be able to return to your original location for any reason, mark your trail by leaving cuts in trees or piles of upturned leaves or stones. To find human habitation, you will need to follow the course of a river or stream. Native villages are normally sited on the banks of rivers. Bear in mind that at night trails and rivers will often be used by animals, many of which will be dangerous.

Movement is easier in the jungle with a map and compass. These "Green Berets" in Vietnam stop to check a map before proceeding.

When sharpening a machete, do it one side at a time on a wet stone. Stroke the blade across the stone in an outward direction only.

Attention must be given regularly to leeches and other parasites, which should be cleared from clothing and skin. Also attend to bites or scratches, which can quickly become infected in the jungle.

A **machete** is one of the best aids to survival in the jungle for hacking down vegetation in your way. When using it, cut at a down and out angle, not flat and level: it requires less effort. When actually working your way through the jungle, follow these rules straight from the "Green Berets":

- Avoid thickets and swamps; move slowly and steadily through dense vegetation.
- Move through the jungle in daylight only.

Over eight million square miles (13 million sq km) of jungle are found in U.S. operational regions around world.

- Use a stick to move vegetation to reduce the possibility of disturbing ant or scorpion nests with your hands or feet.
- Do not grab brush or vines to help you up slopes or over obstacles; their thorns and spines will cause irritation and they may not hold your weight.
- Do not climb over logs if you can walk around them; you may slip and be injured or step on a snake.
- If using a trail, watch for disturbed areas—it may be a trap or pitfall.
- Do not follow a trail that has a rope barrier or grass net across it; it may lead to an animal trap.

Another danger you need to watch out for is **quicksand**. Quicksand is a mixture of sand and water. If you fall into it, you can get trapped and slowly drown. It is usually found near the mouths of large rivers and on flat shores. You can get caught in quicksand very easily. If you do, adopt a spread-eagle position to help disperse your body weight and stop you from sinking. Spread out and swim or pull along the surface. Do not panic; you will sink faster if you do.

In many cases rivers, trails, and ridge lines are the easiest routes to follow, though there are some problems associated with them. Rivers and streams can be overgrown, making them difficult to reach and impossible to sail on the water. Also, the waterways themselves may be infested with leeches and dangerous fish and reptiles. Trails can have traps or animal pits on them, and they can also lead to a dead-end or into swamps or thick bush. Even more hazardous, the vegetation along a ridge may conceal crevices or even extend out past cliff edges.

Despite these problems, waterways offer the best travel routes. If you can, find a stream and travel downstream to a larger body of water. Though following a stream may mean crossing water and cutting through dense vegetation, a stream gives you a definite course that will probably lead to other human beings. It is also a source of food and water.

To cross a stream or river, you must find a place to ford it safely. You will need to choose a suitable spot to cross a river. Look out for a place where you are least in danger of losing your footing. You should have easy access to the water on one side and a way out on the other side. Make sure there is no dangerous wildlife in the area. Climb a tree if necessary, so that you can plan your crossing. When selecting a place, you should look out for a travel course that leads across the current of the flowing water at a 45-degree angle downstream. Choose where the water is shallowest, or where the river is divided up into separate channels that can be negotiated individually, or where there are natural stepping stones. However, avoid areas where water is running rapidly over rocks or where the water looks turbulent. Never attempt to cross a stream directly above, or close to, a rapid waterfall or a deep channel.

When it comes to wading across, the "Green Berets" follow this procedure. Take your clothes off and store them in a plastic bag in your backpack. Keep your boots on to improve your grip on the riverbed. Ensure that your backpack can be taken off easily if you slip—you do not want it to drag you down. Take a sturdy pole with you and push it into the riverbed upstream in order to help break the current. You can brace yourself against the pole. Cross the river at an angle of 45 degrees to the current.

If you are in a team ("Green Berets" usually are), you can make a roped crossing. A roped crossing requires a loop of rope about three times as long as the width of the stream. The strongest person should go across first, with the rope tied around his chest. The other two let out the rope, making sure it does not snag on any obstacles, ready to haul the first person back if necessary. When across, number one unties himself and number two ties the rope around his chest. That person's crossing is monitored by rope holders on both

Tropical rivers are some of the longest on Earth. The biggest is the River Nile, which runs 4,160 miles (6,695 km) down through Africa.

STAY VISIBLE

One of the most important lessons taught by the "Green Berets" is to make yourself visible to would-be rescuers. If you are in an airplane that crashes in the jungle, stay with the aircraft. It is easier to spot the wreckage of a plane than a lone person walking through the jungle.

banks. Number three then crosses, with one person holding the rope taut on the opposite side, and the other ready to help pull the rope if necessary.

Do not try swimming across rivers unless you are confident you can manage the current. (Throw bits of wood into the river to test the strength of the current.) Make sure it is not too cold and that you will not be tangled up in weed, branches, or other obstacles that may be in the river.

If you need to travel some distance, one of the best ways is to build a raft. Special Forces soldiers can produce a good raft in minutes, but they need a lot of practice to perfect it. A raft can be constructed from suitable logs. Test them to make sure they float (at least half in the water and half out). When tying the logs together, cut deep notches into the logs so that the rope or other material you are using to bind them does not slip under the twisting action that will take place in the water.

Place the logs over two crossbars at either end. The longest log goes at the center. Lash the main logs together and then place two bars across the raft at both ends above the other bars. Cut notches in these bars and then lash them together to create pressure on the sides. You can add more crossbars to form a flatter deck. Center boards, which will act like keels and help to stop the raft from drifting sideways, can be pushed down between gaps in the logs and securely lashed.

To steer the raft, make an oar out of a flat piece of wood. Build up the rear of the raft with another couple of logs and then fix the steering oar on top of these in such a way that you will be able to turn it without losing it in the water.

Rafts can speed up jungle travel. Some of the earliest known rafts were simply bundles of reeds used by ancient African communities.

A much simpler sailing device can be made from only two logs and some rope. Place the logs about two feet (60 cm) apart and tie them together, preferably with notches in the logs so that the rope does not slip off. You should then be able to sit between the two logs, with your legs folded over one and your lower back lying against the other. Test the device to make sure your measurements are right and that it works before using it in deeper water.

Rafts should be used with great care. Some jungle waters are so fast they can destroy a raft and drown you in seconds. "Green Berets" use a system of grades to judge whether the water is suitable for a raft:

Grade 1	Moving water with ripples and small waves. Few obstructions. Suitable for rafts.
Grade 2	Easy rapids with waves up to three feet (90 cm) high. Some maneuvering required for a canoe.
Grade 3	Rapids with high waves.
Grade 4	Long difficult rapids that cannot be sailed by open canoes.
Grade 5	Violent rapids.
Grade 6	Very dangerous.

In a raft, anything beyond Grade 1 will probably be unsuitable, and the raft will need to be either carried or abandoned.

However you move through the jungle, you have to be prepared for it to be very slow. If you are in a survival situation, you should always try to attract the attention of rescuers who might be

If you are being rescued by a helicopter, try to clear and flatten an area of about 80 feet (24 m) in diameter for the helicopter to land.

looking for you. This is easier said than done. Jungles have been known to hide entire armies in Vietnam, so it is very difficult for rescue aircraft to spot you. One of the best ways used by the "Green Berets" is smoke. In daylight, smoke can be seen over long distances. Fires should be built, covered, and maintained, ready to be lit the very moment you hear a rescue aircraft's engines. Try to create smoke that will stand out against the background landscape. If you put green leaves, moss, or damp wood on a fire you will get white smoke; rubber or oil-soaked rags on a fire will produce black smoke.

Fire is also very effective for signaling at night. Build a fire that gives out a lot of light using dry logs that burn quickly and brightly.

In a dense jungle, smoke from a green-wood fire can be one of the best ways to let yourself be seen from the air.

NAVIGATING THE DENSE JUNGLE

Moving through the jungle can be incredibly difficult. Thorns and branches snatch at your clothing and the vegetation can be almost impenetrable. Using your machete, hack away at the foliage in front of you to clear yourself a path.

A burning tree is a good way of attracting attention. Trees that produce pitch can be set on fire when green. For other types of trees, place dry wood in the lower branches, and set it on fire. The flames will ignite the tree foliage. Always try to select a tree well away from other trees—you do not want to start a forest fire!

Another "Green Beret" method of attracting attention is by using a reflector. On a sunny day, mirrors, polished metal cups, belt buckles, or other objects will reflect the sun's rays. Angle these toward the sunlight until they give out a bright flash of reflected light. Always practice signaling before you need it. Mirror signals can be seen for 62 miles (100 km) under jungle conditions and over 100 miles (160 km) in other terrain. You may have to climb a tree or a piece of high ground to make sure that you can be seen using the reflector.

Even using signaling, it may take many days in the jungle before you are found, and many days to travel only a few miles. That's why you must learn from the "Green Berets" how to find food and water along the way.

FOOD AND WATER

Water and food are plentiful in tropical regions, and you will be able to survive for a long time in the jungle. However, first you must learn what is safe to eat and what will poison you if you are to avoid disaster.

Although the "Green Beret" in the jungle is not likely to have the same difficulty as the desert survivor in finding sources of water, the problems should not be underestimated. To find water, look for signs of bees, ants, or flies, which all need water. Some birds, such as finches and pigeons, are good indicators of a water source. When they are flying fast and low, they are likely to be heading toward water. When they pause frequently to rest, they are likely to be coming away from water.

Streams are obviously your best source of water. If the stream is fast flowing with a stone and sand bed, the water is likely to be pure, although you can't always be certain. Boil it for 10 minutes or put in **purifying tablets** if in doubt.

A "Green Beret" can also live off water found in plants. Green bamboo often contains trapped water. Shake the bamboo; if a sloshing sound is heard it contains water. Cut off the end of a section that has water in it and drink or pour from the open end. Before you do, look at the inside of the bamboo that contains the

Jungles have many waterfalls. One of the largest is Victoria Falls in Africa. It is 335 feet (108 m) high and over one mile (1.6 km) across.

Bamboo can provide plenty of drinking water when it is split in half, as this Special Forces soldier demonstrates.

water. If the water is clean, you can drink it; if it is brown or black or has any discoloration or fungus present, you must purify it first before drinking.

Banana plants also contain drinkable water. Make a banana well out of the plant stump by cutting out and removing the inner section of the stump. Place a leaf from the banana plant over the bowl while it is filling; this prevents contamination by insects.

Coconuts contain a refreshing liquid. (This milky substance is safe to drink.) The best coconuts to use are green, unripe, and about the size of a grapefruit. The fluid can be drunk in large quantities without harmful effects, although mature coconuts contain amounts of oil, which can cause diarrhea if you drink too much.

Vines also provide water. Nick the vine with your knife and watch the sap run from the cut. If the sap is milky, don't use the vine. If the sap is not milky, cut out a section of the vine, then hold it vertically and watch the liquid as it flows out. If it is clear and colorless, it may be drinkable; if it is milky, it is not. Let some of the liquid flow into the palm of your hand and observe it. If it doesn't change color, taste it. If it tastes like water or is sweet or woody, it should be safe to drink. Liquid with a sour or bitter taste should be

Making a water catcher. A human being needs about five pints (3 liters) of water every day to survive, more if the climate is very hot.

avoided. Do not touch the bark with your mouth because it may make your mouth burn or itch. Finally, in the tropics, plants with large leaves, such as pitcher plants, will catch rainwater. Make sure you pour the water through a filter to remove any insects.

There are many other ways to collect water in the jungle. One particular method used by the "Green Berets" is a vegetation still. Tie a clear plastic bag around a branch so that it covers the leaves at the end. Weigh or tie down the branch so that water from the leaves can drip into the bag as the sun warms it up.

Bamboo is usually found in tropical Asia. Yet one type is also found in the southern United States in areas of marshland or tropical rivers.

A vegetation bag can produce only a small amount of water by extracting water vapor from the plant. Do not rely on it as your main water source.

When it comes to food, "Green Berets" learn to identify hundreds of different types of tropical plants that can be eaten. Here are some of the main ones.

Bamboo

These plants can be found in many parts of the world. The young shoots, up to about a foot (30 cm) in height, can be eaten raw. The fine black hairs along the edge of the leaves of the young shoot are poisonous and should be removed. You can also eat the bamboo seeds when boiled. Bamboo provides all sorts of uses as shelter materials, water carriers, utensils, and tools.

Banana and plantain

Found widely in the humid tropics. These treelike plants have large leaves, and the flowers hang in clusters. You can eat the fruit or the center of the plant either raw or cooked.

The banana plant can grow 10 to 20 feet (3–6 m) high.

Coconut

Found throughout the tropics, mostly near coasts. The white meat inside the fruit can be eaten and the liquid in the

Coconuts float easily on the ocean currents, which explains why they can be found on the coasts of most tropical countries.

unripe fruit is a good thirst-quencher. The palm "cabbage," or sheath from which the leaves protrude, is found at the top of the plant and may be eaten raw, boiled, or roasted.

Mango

The mango tree has shiny leaves. The fruit is oval and turns orange when ripe. It can be eaten raw.

Sweetsop

Widely distributed in tropical regions, this small tree has a fruit with a bumpy shape, which can be eaten raw.

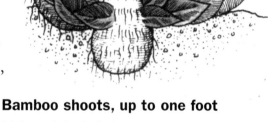

Bamboo shoots, up to one foot (30 cm) in height, can be eaten raw.

Water lily

Found in temperate and subtropical regions in streams and lakes. The seeds and thickened roots of any variety of lily may be eaten boiled or roasted.

Wild yam

Widely distributed in tropical regions, the yam is a ground creeper, and its root can be boiled and eaten like a vegetable.

There are hundreds of thousands of different plants in the jungle, and even the "Green Berets" cannot know them all. You have to be careful because many plants in the jungle are very poisonous and will quickly make you sick. "Green Berets" have a list of general rules for selecting plants to eat:

- Avoid plants with umbrella-shaped flowers, though carrots, celery, and parsley (all edible) are members of this family.
- Avoid all beans and peas.
- If in doubt, avoid all bulbs.
- Avoid all white and yellow berries—they are poisonous. Half of all red berries are poisonous. Blue or black berries are generally safe to eat.
- Single fruits on a stem are considered safe to eat.

A soldier from the Royal Thai Air Force shows U.S. troops the edible portion of a banana tree during Search and Rescue training.

Some mango fruits are only a couple of inches (5 cm) across; other varieties grow to four to five pounds (1.8–2.3 kg) in weight.

• A milky sap indicates a poisonous plant.
• Plants that make your skin itch should not be eaten.
• Plants that grow in water or moist soil are often very tasty.

If you in doubt as to whether you can eat a plant, perform the **Universal Edibility Test**, used widely by the Special Forces. Test each element of a plant at a time by breaking it into separate parts: leaves, stem, and roots. Do not eat for eight hours before starting the test. During this fasting period, hold a sample of the plant on the inside of your elbow or wrist. Wait 15 minutes to see if your skin reacts badly to the plant. (If it does, do not eat the plant.) Also, smell each component of the plant for strong or acidic odors—this is your first clue to edibility.

During the test period, do not eat or drink anything except pure water and the plant to be tested. Select a small portion of the plant. Before putting it in your mouth, put the plant piece on the outer surface of the lip to test for burning or itching. If, after three minutes, there is no reaction, place it on your tongue and hold for 15 minutes. If there is no reaction locally or elsewhere on your body, chew a piece thoroughly and hold it in your mouth for 15 minutes. Do not swallow. If there is no irritation during this time, swallow the food. Wait eight hours. If any ill effects occur, induce vomiting (by putting your fingers down your throat) and drink plenty of pure water. If no bad effects occur, eat half a cup of the same plant prepared the same way. Wait another eight hours; if no ill effects are suffered the plant as prepared is safe to eat.

Warning: Fungi should not be used in the taste test. Deadly fungi

A VARIETY OF WILDLIFE

Fortunately for the survivor, the tropics have an extremely rich wildlife population. Because of this, the "Green Beret" soldier should never go hungry in the jungle. There are literally millions of different species of plants and animals to be found. If you were to stand in the tropical rainforest for only 10 minutes, you might see a plant or creature that had never before been seen.

do not taste unpleasant and the symptoms of poisoning may not appear until several hours after eating. There is no antidote for fungal poisoning, so either know exactly what fungi are safe to eat or leave well alone.

Jungle animals

Of course, plants are not the only food in the jungle. There are also many animals. Animals in the rainforest tend to be small and tree-dwelling, which can make capturing them difficult. The few larger

The most powerful snares today are usually designed to trap wolves and they can take 800 pounds (362 kg) of pressure before they snap.

rainforest animals include the elephant and the okapi, a shy and rarely seen relative of the giraffe.

In Africa there are two kinds of pig living in the forest, the bush pig, or red river hog, and the giant forest hog. In Asia, there are three kinds of pig: the common wild boar, the bearded pig, and the babirussa, which has upward-growing tusks. In South America, there are two kinds of **peccary** living in the rainforest, though only the white-tailed peccary is a true tropical rainforest dweller. All these animals can be dangerous and, realistically, should be hunted only with a rifle or a good spear.

Animals move along trails in the jungle, and that is where you should place your traps. The animals you can hope to trap are hedgehogs, porcupines, anteaters, mice, wild pigs, deer, wild cattle, squirrels, rats, and monkeys. Although they are all edible, you are strongly advised to avoid the following animals: tigers, rhinoceros, water buffalo, elephants, crocodiles, caimans, and cobras (some of

The ocelot is a beautiful creature, but its numbers are declining. In Texas, the ocelot is endangered, even though trading in its fur is illegal.

which spit poison into the eyes). They are all dangerous and could kill you. Also avoid all brilliantly colored or strong-smelling frogs; they are poisonous. Reptiles are abundant in the jungle and should be considered a food source. Treat all snakes as poisonous and kill them with a heavy blow to the back of the head.

There are many members of the cat family in tropical regions. The ocelot, which has a dark-spotted, yellow gray coat, is common in the jungles of Central and Latin America. It is small, lean, and savage, weighs around 40 pounds (18 kg) when fully grown, and is approximately three feet (90 cm) long. The leopard is also found in the tropics, though this powerful beast is not easy to trap. Unlike lions and tigers, it can climb trees easily. You therefore cannot take refuge up a tree if you become the hunted! On a smaller scale, ants, grubs, grasshoppers, and crickets are also edible, though the wings and legs should be avoided. Grubs can be split and broiled over a fire.

DEALING WITH SHARKS

Watch out for sharks near the coasts of jungle areas. If you are in the water and sharks come toward you, shout loudly and smack your hands on the surface to try to scare them away. If there is a group of you, form a tight circle for added safety. Sharks are also not very good at turning quickly, so if one goes for you, wait until the last second and then swim quickly to one side. "Green Berets" *never* swim directly away from a shark. It will sense fear and come after you.

Many tropical areas are near the sea. If you are near a seashore, fish, crabs, lobsters, crayfish, and octopuses can be a part of your diet. Try to spear, net, or catch them before they move off into deep water. Snails and limpets cling to rocks and seaweed above the low-water mark. Pry them off with a knife. Mussels form dense colonies in rock pools, on logs, or at the base of boulders. However, mussels are poisonous during the summer. The safest fish to eat are those from the open sea or deep water beyond the reef.

The abundance of jungle life makes it one of the easiest survival situations to find food and water. Yet the "Green Beret" is not complacent. The jungle can be a dangerous place, and it is a good idea to build a shelter to protect yourself.

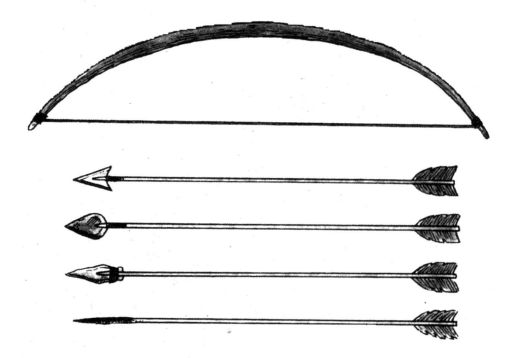

The bow and arrow is good for hunting. In medieval England, an archer could fire six arrows per minute to a range of 600 feet (180 m).

U.S. forces have traditionally had better food than others. In the Civil War, soldiers received coffee and sugar as part of their rations.

SHELTER

Though the jungle is usually warm, the "Green Beret" will often build a shelter at night. A good shelter will help you keep clean and protect you from animals and insects.

In tropical jungle and rainforests, the ground is damp and teeming with insects, leeches, and reptiles. You therefore do not want to sleep on it. (Snakes will be attracted to your body warmth during the night—you may wake up to find one curled around your stomach!) "Green Berets" make a raised shelter that will let them sleep off the ground. If you can, you should build a shelter on a high spot in a clearing well away from pools of water, where the ground will be drier, there will be fewer insects, and it will be easier to signal for help.

When clearing a site for a shelter, remember to clear away underbrush and dead vegetation. Crawling insects will not be able to approach as easily due to lack of cover, and snakes will be less likely to come toward you. One more thing: remember to look above you when you have chosen your shelter site. You do not want to be below dead wood that comes crashing down in the next heavy wind, or a hornets' or wasps' nest.

If you are in a swamp, you will want to build a raised shelter to prevent you from getting wet. Keep on the lookout for four trees

An expertly built Special Forces shelter. It includes a fireplace, a sleeping platform, and a thatched roof.

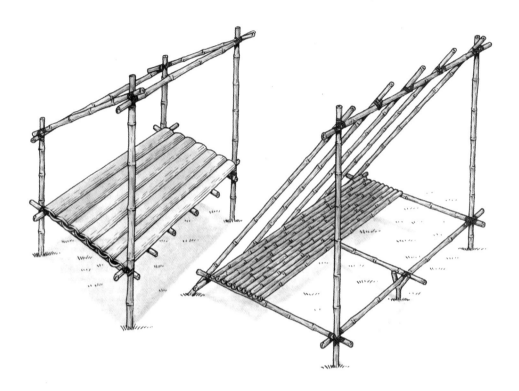

Bamboo is the easiest material from which to make platform shelters. The sloped roofs mean that rainwater runs straight off them.

clustered in a rectangle that can support your weight. Cut two poles from any other trees and fasten them to the trees (do not use rotten sticks), and then lay more poles across them. Cover the top of the frame with broad leaves or grass to form a sleeping surface. When in a swamp, remember to look out for tide marks on surrounding trees to ensure you build your shelter high enough.

A different type of shelter is the banana leaf **A-frame**. This makes an excellent rain shelter. Construct an A-shape framework (like a wigwam) and cover it with a good thickness of palm or other broad-leafed plants. Make sure the leaves are overlapping.

PROTECTION FROM MOSQUITOES

Mosquito nets are excellent items to take into the jungle with you. Drape it around your shelter to stop yourself from getting bitten by insects during the night. This will mean you get a good night's sleep and it will reduce your chances of getting a disease.

On any type of shelter, you can use split bamboo to make a bed or roofing: cut the stem in half and lay the pieces so that they interlock with each other. You can also flatten split bamboo and use it for lining walls or shelving. Large leaves such as palm and atap

There are about five million insects in one square acre (4,000 sq m) of soil, so it is essential to keep your shelter off the ground.

TIPS FOR LIVING IN YOUR SHELTER

- Make a separate toilet well away from the main shelter—it will attract insects.
- If you build a fire, make sure that the smoke can escape from your shelter so that it doesn't poison you.
- If you are staying in the shelter for some time, repair any damage as soon as it happens.

(barbed vine) can be woven together to create a roof and walls for the shelter as well as bedding. Be careful when handling bamboo, because it can split suddenly when cut and send out sharp splinters. Leaves can be razor-sharp and can inflict painful cuts if not handled carefully.

Once you have made your shelter, you need somewhere to sleep. One of the best beds the "Green Berets" use is a hammock. A hammock can be made quickly if you have a **poncho** or similar type of material and rope. A hammock may be tied between two trees or three or more for greater stability.

Because many jungles are found on the coast, the survivor should also know how to make a seashore shelter. When doing this, be sure how far the tide comes in before you build it. Dig into the sheltered side of a sand dune to protect the shelter from the wind. Clear a flat area large enough for you to lie down in and for storing equipment. After the area has been cleared, build a heavy framework from driftwood that will support the sand. Then make walls for the side and top. You must use strong materials, such as boards or driftwood. Remember to leave an opening for a door.

Cover the entire roof with some sort of material to prevent sand from sifting through small holes in the walls and roof. This material should be fairly thick and hard-wearing. Then cover the roof with 6 to 12 inches (15–30 cm) of sand to provide protection from the wind and moisture. Finally, make a door for the shelter.

Once you are fed, watered, and sheltered, you will be able to survive for as long as you have strength in you. However, "Green Berets" have to have their eyes open constantly for the many dangers that surround them in the jungle. This is what we will learn about in our next chapter.

Waterproof shelters are essential in wet tropical areas, some of which experience up to 39 inches (1,000 cm) of rainfall each year.

DANGERS

Some of the world's most dangerous animals live in the jungle. The "Green Berets" teach you not to panic when you meet them, and show you how to get out of their way before they strike.

Most people imagine that the main dangers in the jungle come from snakes and large wild animals. While it is true that both are dangerous, the Special Forces soldier will tell you the bigger danger to the survivor is from insects that transmit diseases or have poisonous bites or stings. Spending much of his or her time stationed in the jungle, the "Green Beret" is trained to know what animals and insects should be treated with caution. Failure to do so could be a matter of life and death.

There are several types of dangerous or unpleasant insects and spiders which you will need to avoid in the jungle.

Ants
Red ants nest in the twigs of trees and shrubs and will bite viciously if disturbed.

Centipedes
Centipedes are mostly harmless, but some species can cause swellings and infections if they bite you.

This soldier is looking down the barrel of a 7.62-mm caliber M60 machine gun, which can fire 200 bullets in less than 30 seconds.

Hornets, bees, and wasps

These can be found in a variety of forms worldwide. They are best left undisturbed, so stay away from their nests and do not build shelters near them. Stings from several hornets can kill. Wasps tend to attack moving targets. However, if a swarm is attacking, run through dense undergrowth—this makes it more difficult for them to follow you.

Leeches

Leeches are bloodsucking, sluglike, insects that can drop onto human skin and feed. Do not just pull them off you. The best methods of removal are by touching it with fire (such as a lit match or smoldering piece of wood) or by sprinkling the creature with salt. These techniques should make the creature shrivel and drop off you. Clean the wound.

Mosquitoes

Mosquitoes are actually the world's most dangerous creature. This is because certain types of mosquito in the tropics carry a disease

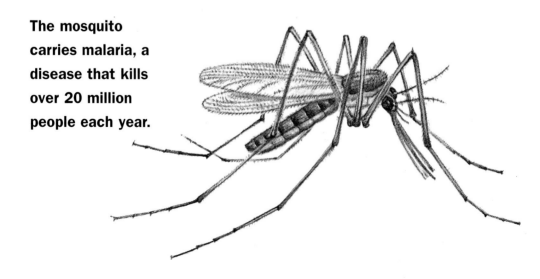

The mosquito carries malaria, a disease that kills over 20 million people each year.

This man is well protected against a bee swarm. Stinging insects come in huge varieties—there are 20,000 species of wasp alone.

called **malaria**. When they bite you to feed off your blood, they can give you the disease. Twenty million people around the world die of malaria each year. Always use a **mosquito net**, if available, when you sleep. If not, make one with cloth, a parachute, or large leaves. Particularly at night, tuck the legs of your trousers into your socks and your shirtsleeves into your gloves. Keep a fire smoking at night, and keep away from swampy or stagnant areas, because this is where mosquitoes breed.

Scorpions

These are dangerously poisonous. They can be found in tropical jungles and are usually darker than the desert varieties. Some jungle varieties can be up to eight inches (20 cm) long.

Black widow or hourglass spider

These are dangerously poisonous. Found in warm areas world-wide, they are small and dark with hourglass markings on the abdomen.

Funnelweb

These are deadly poisonous spiders. Found in Australia, they are small and black with short legs.

Tarantula

These are poisonous, large, and hairy spiders. Generally of American origin, they are sluggish but capable of biting sharply through most materials. Their poison is not as dangerous as their appearance suggests, but it will cause skin irritation.

REPELLING INSECTS

Insects can make your life a misery in the jungle. However, they do not like smoke. Build a nice smoky fire in the middle of your camp. Though it might make your throat a bit dry, you will prefer this to insect attacks.

Ticks

Ticks are common in the tropics. They are small, round insects that feed on blood by biting into the skin, whereupon their jaws lock very firmly. Do not attempt to pull one off, since it will leave its jaws embedded in your skin. Heat, gasoline, or alcohol should make it drop off. If you have caught an animal such as a pig, be careful that ticks do not jump off the dead animal onto you.

When dealing with insects, the "Green Berets" follow a set of rules that protect them from getting bitten. Use **insect repellent**, if you have it, on all exposed areas of the skin and on all clothing openings.

Tarantulas have a body length of up to two inches (5 cm) and a leg span of up to five inches (12.5 cm).

Wear clothing all the time, especially at night. Cover your arms and legs. Wear gloves and a mosquito head net if possible to give you extra protection. Camp well away from swamps. Sleep under mosquito netting if you have it. If not, smear mud on your face to keep away the insects.

There are many types of **venomous** snakes in tropical areas, including vipers, cobras, tropical rattlesnakes, mambas, and kraits. Some cobras can spit poison as well as bite. If the poison gets into your eyes or an open cut, wash out the wound immediately with water or, in an emergency, with urine. Snakes will not usually bother

Snakes are formidable hunters. They spend 70 percent of their lives engaged in tracking down, killing, or eating their prey.

you, but do not handle or provoke any snake and treat all snakes as poisonous. Note: a few tropical snakes, such as the bushmaster and mamba, will attack for no apparent reason.

The main types of dangerous snakes that "Green Berets" are trained to identify are listed below:

Gaboon viper
Appearance: patterns of blacks, browns, and blues.
Length: four to five feet (1.2–1.5 m).
Temperament: will coil and strike quickly when approached.

Puff adder
Appearance: light or dark-brown color, with white or yellow angled stripes.
Length: three to four feet (90–120 cm)
Temperament: strikes with lightning speed if provoked.

Rhinoceros viper
Appearance: large, heavy bodied, and colored in pinks, blues, and greens.
Length: two to four feet (60–120 cm)
Temperament: strikes with lightning speed when approached.

Bushmaster
Appearance: dark brown or tan, with some pink colors and black blotches along its back.
Length: six to seven feet (1.8–2.1 m)

Temperament: may remain motionless until touched, will attack viciously if cornered. May sometimes attack for no reason.

Cottonmouth

Appearance: young are colored with bands of copper, light-brown, and dark-brown. In adults, the bands may be faint to total black.
Length: three to four feet (90–120 cm)

Temperament: fierce, do not annoy them.

Green tree pit viper
Appearance: brilliant green in color.
Length: two to three feet. (60–90 cm)
Temperament: not aggressive, but because they live in shrubs and trees they are difficult to see.

Jumping pit viper
Appearance: brown/black.
Length: two to three feet (60–90 cm)

An army survival instructor teaches U.S. troops how to deal with a cobra if encountered in the jungle.

Temperament: will strike readily, often with such force that its body will leave the ground.

Malayan pit viper
Appearance: reddish brown back, dark brown crossbands, and pinkish brown on the sides.
Length: two to three feet (60–90 cm)
Temperament: calm, but if stepped on, it will bite. It bites many people each year, largely because it lives in populated areas.

Tropical rattlesnake
Appearance: dark brown with diamond-shaped markings down its back and dark stripes along its neck.
Length: four to five feet (1.2–1.5 m)
Temperament: always ready to strike, coiling and elevating its head high above the coil. It may not rattle its tail before doing so.

Wagler's pit viper
Appearance: green-colored with black-edged scales. Has a stout body.
Length: two to three feet (60–90 cm)
Temperament: placid.

Krait
Appearance: bright grayish to black, with narrow white crossbands, and a white belly.
Length: three to six feet (90–180 cm)

Temperament: not aggressive, but its venom is deadly. Native of Pakistan, India, southeastern Asia, and adjacent islands.

Coral snakes
Appearance: colored with blacks, reds, and yellows. Has a small head.
Length: one to three feet (30–90 cm)
Temperament: placid, will not bite unless stepped on or picked up.

King cobra
Appearance: olive or light brown, these large cobras can stand three to four feet (90–120 cm) off the ground. Extends hood when it does so.
Length: seven to nine feet (2.1–2.7 m)
Temperament: aggressive, especially when guarding eggs.

Mambas
Appearance: green or dark gray with a small head and slender body.
Length: five to seven feet (1.5–2.1 m)
Temperament: quick to strike; have been known to attack without provocation.

Boomslang
Appearance: green, brown, or black and very slender. It inflates its throat when alarmed.
Length: four to five feet (1.3–1.5 m)
Temperament: aggressive.

Taipan

Appearance: light or dark brown, with yellowish brown sides and belly.

Length: 11 feet (3.5 m)

Temperament: ferocious.

Of course, the "Green Berets" have a set of rules that help them avoid being bitten by snakes: Be careful where you step; snakes are often sluggish and can be stepped on—that's when they usually bite. Since some snakes live in trees, be careful when you pick fruit or part bushes. Do not taunt, corner, or handle a snake. Use a stick to turn over stones, not your hands. Wear strong boots if you have them— many snake fangs cannot stab through boot leather. Always check bedding, clothes, and packs before putting them on—snakes can crawl inside them for

A "Green Beret" carrying a Colt Commando rifle, a shortened version of the M16.

warmth. If you encounter a snake, stay calm and back away. In most cases the snake will want to escape. To kill a snake, use a long stick and strike it on the back of the head. Make sure you kill it; a wounded snake is ferocious.

Snakes and insects are not the only animals you have to watch out for in the jungle. For example, all tropical areas contain wild pigs. These pigs have an aggressive nature and should be treated with caution. Some small pigs travel in herds of 5 to 15, and in these numbers they can easily deal with a jaguar, cougar, or human. It is

Despite their great size, some crocodiles can move as fast as humans, reaching speeds of 18 miles per hour (29 km/h).

best to try to kill them at a distance with a spear. Do not try to tackle them yourself; their tusks can inflict severe injuries to your legs.

The water also holds many dangers. Crocodiles and alligators often lie on banks or float like logs with just their eyes above the water. Be careful when crossing deep streams, bathing, or getting near water. Avoid these animals at all times; their tails can inflict a lethal blow, and their jaws can crush you. If you have to get into the water, move slowly. Thrashing around will attract them.

"Green Berets" are very careful of streams in the dry season when water levels are low. South American rivers can contain piranhas. These are long, solid fish with razor-sharp teeth and they will attack in large numbers. Sharks have been known to attack humans in saltwater estuaries, bays, or lagoons. Barracuda have also been known to attack in murky or clouded waters.

Do not walk barefoot on coral reefs, which can cut your feet to ribbons. Fine needles from sponges and sea urchins may get into your skin. You may also tread on a stonefish, which will cause you agonizing pain, even death. Always use a stick to probe dark holes. Slide your feet along the bottom of muddy or sandy bottoms of rivers and seashores to avoid stepping on stingrays or other sharp-spiked animals.

No matter how careful you are, the jungle contains enough dangerous plants and animals to make poisoning a real possibility. Even the "Green Berets" are not immune to a snake or sniper bite. That's why they are trained in jungle first aid, the lesson of our next chapter.

FIRST AID

When bitten by a snake or dangerous spider, the "Green Beret" must work fast to stop the injury from becoming life-threatening. A calm head and the right techniques are required to deliver jungle first aid.

Among the many dangers in the jungle, plants and animals can deliver powerful poisons. In fact, animal poisons are some of the most lethal chemicals known to humankind. Their effects are highly varied. A jellyfish sting, for example, will feel like a bad bee sting, but if you tread on the spine of an Indo-Pacific cone shell, you will be lucky to live. It is impossible here to run through the poisonous qualities of all the world's deadly or harmful creatures. The "Green Berets" respond to a case of animal or plant poisoning in the best way they know how, even if they are not sure what caused it.

All animal bites are dangerous even if no poison is injected. This is because animal teeth contain lots of harmful bacteria. Once you are bitten, it is very likely that a wound will become seriously infected. Some of the most dangerous bites in this regard are those of monkeys—clean them thoroughly with water immediately after they happen. However, we will concentrate here on what to do if you are bitten by a poisonous snake.

"Green Berets" treat an injury. The plastic bag contains a salt-water solution, which is used to replace fluids lost by the injured man.

Snake poison has different results according to the type of snake. In some cases, the only injury will be swollen and torn skin. However, in other cases the symptoms are far more serious. The breathing and heart can stop, victims can fall unconscious, or they may be paralyzed.

A Special Forces soldier practices survival first aid on a "casualty" with a simulated arm injury.

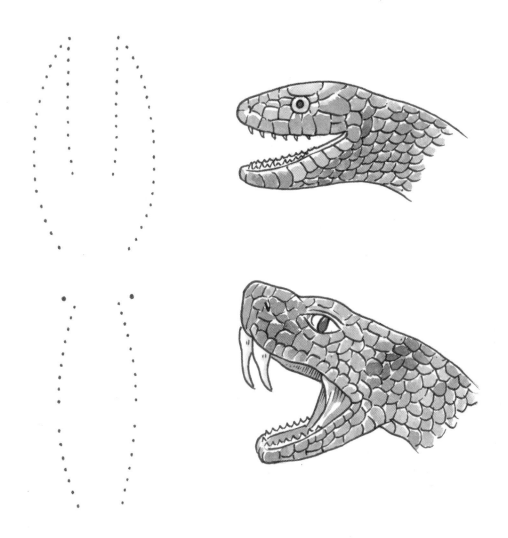

Poisonous and nonpoisonous snakes have different bite marks. Only the bottom snake here is poisonous, as indicated by fang marks.

If someone has been bitten by a snake, have a look at the bite marks. Sometimes this can tell you whether the snake was poisonous or not. If there are one or two larger puncture wounds at the front of the bite, separate from the rest, the chances are it was poisonous. Do not, however, assume that all bites from

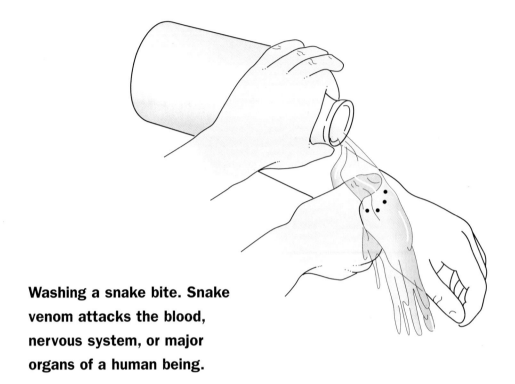

Washing a snake bite. Snake venom attacks the blood, nervous system, or major organs of a human being.

poisonous snakes mean that venom has actually been injected. Snakes often bite out of fear rather than for food, so they do not actually inject. You will know if they have because of the immediate swelling of the wound site and the victim will quickly become very ill.

Once the victim has been bitten, even if you think they are all right, your main priority above all is to get the person rescued. Try to find out what type of snake did the biting. If you can't tell what it is, make sure that at least you jot down some of its features. You can give this information to doctors and they can then give the right medical treatment. Even for "Green Berets," there is little you can do to stop the effect of the poison itself—once it is in, you cannot take it out. Your priority should be slowing down the circulation of the poison around the victim's body. Try to calm the victim as much as possible to slow the heartbeat. Wash the wound site with soap and water to remove any poison remaining on the surface.

Then tie a tight bandage around the bitten limb (if it is a limb that has been bitten) above the place where the victim has been bitten. For example, if the hand has been bitten, tie the bandage just above

A nurse and "Green Beret" soldier treat an injury in Vietnam. Feet are one of the most commonly injured body parts in the jungle.

the elbow. This should be tight, but not tight enough to cut off the blood flow. You can check this by pinching the finger- or toenails. If they go white when you pinch them but go red again when you let go, then the blood flow is fine. If they stay white when you let go, then it means blood is not flowing to the nails and it is too tight. Loosen the bandage. The effect of the bandage is to slow down the flow of the venom through the body. However, if you find it difficult to control the pressure and are cutting off circulation, do away with it immediately.

A different type of poisoning the "Green Beret" may have to treat occurs when someone has swallowed something poisonous, usually

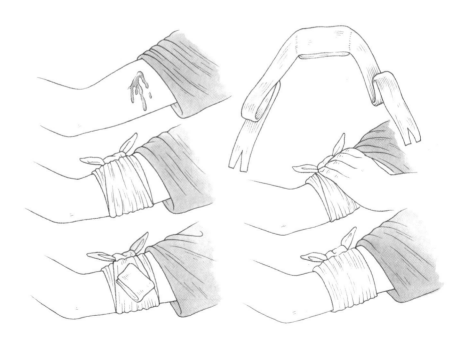

Protect a bleeding arm by putting a pad over the wound and bandaging around it. Tie the bandage ends to keep it in place. For heavy bleeding, repeat with a second pad and bandage.

a dangerous plant. In this situation, your biggest decision is whether or not to make the person vomit. This can be good because it brings up the dangerous substance from the person's stomach rather than leaving it in there to keep poisoning. If you are at home and someone has poisoned themselves, you should not usually do this because the professional medical services will be able to make the right diagnosis and give better treatments. However, in the jungle you often do not have that luxury, so the poison should be brought out of the person as quickly as possible.

There is one exception. Do not make the person vomit if the poisonous substance swallowed is caustic, corrosive, and chemical in nature. Bringing these substances up can burn the patient's throat again. But for general poisoning from plants, food, or medicine, make the person vomit by getting them to put their

TREATING SNAKE BITES

Whatever you might see at the movies, never try to suck out the poison from a snake bite. This will only make things worse for the victim and could result in your being poisoned too. In addition to snakes that bite, there are snakes that spit. These spray venom over some distances, often at the eyes. The effect can be very painful, and you should wash your eyes thoroughly with water immediately. The best advice is to stay clear of snakes in the first place.

finger down their throat. This should bring up the stomach contents almost instantly. Then try to get the victim to professional help as quickly as you can.

Another type of poisoning occurs when poisons are placed onto the skin. This is often caused by brushing against plants that have poisonous thorns or leaves. The effect can be swollen, red skin, and a feeling that the skin is burning. The best way to treat this is to pour lots of fresh water over the wound to wash away the poison. Do not touch the poisoned area with your own hands. Then wrap a bandage over the injury to let it heal. Also wash or remove any clothing that may have been in contact with the poison.

Though nonpoisonous animals do not have deadly venom, they can inflict a serious bite that results in lots of bleeding. If someone is bleeding heavily—whether or not it is from a bite—then you have to act quickly. The "Green Berets" have the following response to someone with a bleeding injury: Lay the victim down. (Find an area that is free of insect nests before you do.) Take away clothing around the place that is bleeding. Apply a forceful pressure directly over the bleeding with a large clean piece of material. In a real emergency, if you don't have this material, use your hand or fingers instead.

Keep the pressure constant until the bleeding is under control. This should happen in about 15 minutes. If the bleeding is from a limb, raise it high during treatment to reduce the amount of blood flowing there. Once the bleeding has stopped, leave the pad of material in place (unless it was originally very dirty). Then bandage it in place. Do not bandage it too tightly because this may restrict circulation to the site, which is vital to the wound's healing. Keep an eye on the bandage to check for more bleeding. If this happens, place another pad on the top and bandage that into place. Also make sure you give the victim plenty to drink, but give only small sips at a time.

Knowing how to deal with bleeding and poisoning are some of the most important first-aid techniques to use in the jungle. But remember, even "Green Berets" will call for help if someone is badly hurt.

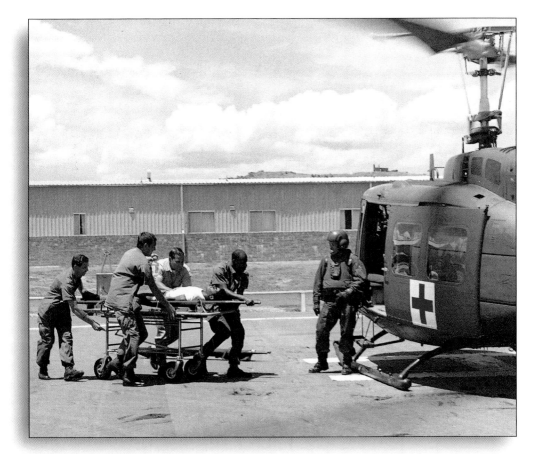

American soldiers were faced with the need for medical attention on a daily basis during the Vietnam War.

GLOSSARY

A-frame A shelter built over a pointed frame of branches, like a wigwam.

Bright Light "Green Beret" missions to rescue American soldiers from the hands of the communists in Vietnam.

Bushfires Fast-burning fires that ignite among very dry grassland and forests.

Counterinsurgency A type of warfare aimed at defeating guerrilla soldiers through sabotage, ambushes, and intelligence.

Desert Shield The operation during the Gulf War to protect Saudi Arabia from invasion by Iraq.

Fast-attack vehicle A special, heavily armed buggy used by the Green Berets during the Gulf War.

Insect repellent Special chemicals that keep insects away from human skin.

Korean War A war between North and South Korea between 1950 and 1953, which involved the United States and many other nations.

Leeches Bloodsucking sluglike creatures that drop from trees and can attach themselves to human skin to feed.

Machete A long-bladed knife used for chopping plants and branches.

Malaria A very dangerous disease passed to humans in the tropics through the bite of an infected mosquito.

Monsoon A windy season in India and the Far East that often brings huge amounts of rain.

Mosquito net A net draped around a bed to stop mosquitoes from getting close enough to bite.

Peccary A small piglike mammal.

Poncho A blanket with a slit in the middle that can be slipped over the head and worn as a sleeveless garment.

Purifying tablets Tablets that are dropped into unclean water to make it safe for humans to drink.

Quicksand A dangerous mix of sand and water in which people can drown if they fall into it.

Rainforest Forests in South America, Asia, Africa, and even tropical Australia, which have a lot of rainfall and a hot, steamy climate.

Savannas Broad, grassy plains with trees spaced far apart.

SFGA Special Forces Group (Airborne).

Swamps Muddy, watery areas that fall into three types: saltwater, mangrove, and freshwater swamps.

Universal Edibility Test A special test designed to see whether unknown plants are poisonous or not.

Venomous Poisonous, referring to snake bites.

Viet Cong The guerrilla soldiers who fought against South Vietnam and its allies (including the United States) during the Vietnam War.

Vietnam War A war in the Far East, in which the US fought between 1965 and 1973.

EQUIPMENT REQUIREMENTS

Headwear
Hat with wide brim
Arab headdress
Scarf/neckcloth (to soak up sweat
    and control temperature)
Face protector (to keep insects
away)

Clothing
Long-sleeved shirts (preferably
    white to reflect the heat)
Shorts
Many pairs of socks
Dark sunglasses

Footwear
Walking boots
Spare shoelaces

Load-carrying equipment
Backpack
Small carry sack

Survival equipment
Medical pack
Sunblock
Mess pack and knife/fork/spoon
Water bottle and mug

Survival knife
Lockable/retractable knife
Tent
Sleeping bag
Sleeping mat
Machete
Shovel/spade (foldable)
Compass
Watch
Chronograph
Flares
Signaling mirror (heliograph)
Binoculars
Map case
Wash pack
Matches
Flint and steel firelighter
Snare wire
Whistle
Wire saw
Candle
Needles
Water purification tablets

CHRONOLOGY

July 9, 1942	1st Special Service Force formed, a joint U.S.–Canadian undercover operations unit.
June 18, 1952	10th Special Forces Group (Airborne)—SFGA—is created at Fort Bragg, North Carolina, by Colonel Aaron Bank.
1955–1969	Special Forces troops help to train elite units in various Latin American armies.
December 10, 1956	The U.S. Army Special Warfare School is created to train elite soldiers.
September 21, 1961	The 5th Special Forces Group is activated at Fort Bragg.
1961–1973	U.S. Special Forces take part in the Vietnam War, going deep into enemy territory to fight the Viet Cong and the North Vietnamese Army. They also help Vietnamese civilians to defend themselves against communist troops. In 1970 "Green Berets" are awarded the Civic Action Medal for this work.
1981	"Green Berets" go on undercover training missions into war-torn Nicaragua.
1983	"Green Berets" are deployed during the U.S. invasion of Grenada—they are among the first troops to enter.
1986	Special Forces units in action in El Salvador.
1990–1991	The Gulf War. Special Forces are used to destroy Iraqi targets such as radar stations and missiles.
1993	U.S. Special Forces are transported to former Yugoslavia to conduct reconnaissance missions.
1990s–2001	"Green Beret" teams regularly conduct training missions into Colombia to help government forces fight the illegal drug industry.
September 11, 2001	In response to terrorist attacks, U.S. military, including Special Forces are put on the highest military alert since the Cuban Missile Crisis.

RECRUITMENT INFORMATION

The Special Forces take only people who are already soldiers. They:
- Must be U.S. male citizens.
- Must volunteer for airborne training and complete that training prior to coming to the Special Forces Qualification Course.
- Must have a minimum GT score of 110; waiverable to 100.
- Must be a High School graduate or have GED equivalent.
- Must be able to swim 170 feet (50 m) wearing boots and battle dress uniform (BDU) at the start of the Special Forces Qualification Course.
- Must score a minimum of 229 points on the Army physical fitness test (APFT). This is made up of three exercises: push-ups, sit-ups, and a two-mile run. Each discipline affords a maximum score of 100. (The number of repetitions and time for the run varies according to the height and weight of the applicant).
- Must pass the Special Forces physical.
- In terms of rank, they must be Special (E-4) through Sergeant First Class (E7) or a promotable First Lieutenant or Captain.

Selection for Special Forces training is based on a 25-day Special Forces Assessment and Selection (SFAS) course. If you pass, you go onto proper Special Forces training, which lasts up to one year, plus four to six months for language training and three weeks for the Survival, Evasion, Resistance, and Escape (SERE) Course.

If you want to find out more about the U.S. Special Forces, go to your nearest U.S. Army recruiting office or visit the following websites:
http://www.goarmy.com
http://www.specialforces.net
http://specialoperations.com
http://www.users.aol.com/armysof1/SpecialForces.html
http://www.members.nbci.com/raymondluk
http://www.20thspecialforcesgroup.com

FURTHER READING

Davies, Barry. *SAS Jungle Survival.* London: Virgin Publishing, 2001.

Halberstadt, Hans. *The Green Berets.* Wiltshire, England: The Crowood Press, 1999.

Halberstadt, Hans. *War Stories of the Green Berets.* Osceola, Wis.: Motorbooks International, 1994.

Kelly, F.J. *Green Berets in Vietnam, 1961–71.* London: Brassey's Macmillan, 1991.

Stilwell, Alexander. *The Encyclopedia of Survival Techniques.* New York: Lyons Press, 2000.

Streissguth, Thomas. *The Green Berets (Serving Your Country).* Minnetonka, Minn.: Capstone Press, 1995.

Walden, John. *Jungle Travel and Survival.* New York: Lyons Press, 2001.

Wiseman, John. *The SAS Survival Handbook.* New York: HarperCollins, 2001.

ABOUT THE AUTHOR

Dr. Chris McNab has written and edited numerous books on military history and elite forces survival. His publications to date include *German Paratroopers of World War II*, *The Illustrated History of the Vietnam War*, *First Aid Survival Manual*, and *Special Forces Endurance Techniques*, as well as many articles and features in other works. Forthcoming publications include books on the SAS, while Chris's wider research interests lie in literature and ancient history. Chris lives in South Wales, U.K.

INDEX

References in italics refer to illustrations